At Tea

Making
Memories
With Friends

A Special Gift

To

My dear friend Shirley

From

Donita

Date

January 1996

Little Ribbons of Love

Afternoon Tea

Angels: Ever In Our Midst

Flowers for a Friend

Sisters: So Much We Share

Afternoon Tea

Brownlow
Brownlow Publishing Company, Inc.

*There are few hours in life
more agreeable than the hour
dedicated to the ceremony
known as afternoon tea.*

HENRY JAMES

Should I, after tea and cake and ices,
Have the strength to force the moment
to its crisis?

T. S. ELIOT

Live your life and forget your age.

FRANK BERING

Although we travel the world over to find the beautiful, we must carry it with us, or we find it not.

RALPH WALDO EMERSON

Living means making your life
a memorable experience.

ANONYMOUS

Offer hospitality to one another....
Each one should use whatever gift
he has received to serve others.

1 PETER 4:9,10

There is a great deal of poetry
and fine sentiment
in a chest of tea.

Ralph Waldo Emerson

Friends choose each other, try each other out, don't have to go too fast at first, don't have to promise to have lunch every day from now to eternity.

MARGARET MEAD

If the world seems cold to you,

Kindle fires to warm it!

If the world's a wilderness,

Go, build houses in it!

LUCY LARCOM

What an angel a woman can be, in doing, feeling, and suffering!

MRS. JAMESON

Sooner or later you've heard all your best friends have to say. Then comes the tolerance of real love.

NED ROREM

When you rise in the morning,
form a resolution to make the day a
happy one to a fellow-creature.

SYDNEY SMITH

Better to be deprived of food
for three days than of tea for one.

CHINESE PROVERB

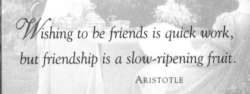

*Wishing to be friends is quick work,
but friendship is a slow-ripening fruit.*

ARISTOTLE

To me, fair friend, you can never
    be old,
For as you were when first your eye
I ey'd,
        Such seems your beauty still.

WILLIAM SHAKESPEARE

When a person finds no peace
within himself, it is useless
to seek it elsewhere.

To be unselfish in everything,
especially in love and friendship,
was my highest pleasure, my maxim,
my discipline.

GOETHE

In China, long ago, tea was
an ingredient in immortality potions.
Even today, some maintain that
tea drinking helps one to live
to a ripe old age.

*T*he best and most beautiful things
in the world cannot be seen
or even touched. They must be felt
with the heart.

HELEN KELLER

It is very easy to forgive others their mistakes; it takes more grit and gumption to forgive them for having witnessed your own.

JESSAMYN WEST

The Dutch brought the first tea to Europe. The first evidence of tea in England was in 1658.

It is great to have friends when one is young, but indeed it is still more so when you are getting old. When we are young, friends are, like everything else, a matter of course. In the old days we know what it means to have them.

EDVARD GRIEG

Music washes away from the soul
the dust of everyday life.

AUERBACH

You can't reason with your heart;
it has its own laws, and thumps
about things which the intellect scorns.

MARK TWAIN

My Prayer

Oh Lord, I would delight in thee,
And on thy care depend;
To thee in every trouble flee,
My best, my nearest Friend

A MOTHER'S HYMN BOOK, 1836

Happiness seems made to be shared.

JEAN RACINE

Friendship is like two clocks keeping time.

ANONYMOUS

Good words are worth much and cost little.

GEORGE HERBERT

For whoever knows how to return a kindness he has received must be a friend above all price.

SOPHOCLES

Because of a friend, life is a little stronger, fuller, more gracious thing for the friend's existence, whether he be near or far. If the friend is close at hand, that is best; but if he is far away he still is there to think of, to wonder about, to hear from, to write to, to share life and experience with, to serve, to honor, to admire, to love.

ARTHUR CHRISTOPHER BENSON

Afternoon Tea

Anna, the seventh Duchess of
Bedford, began the institution known
as "Afternoon Tea" in England during
the 1840's. She commonly had
"a sinking feeling" in the late afternoon

because the customary lunch was only a few snacks and dinner was not served until eight o'clock. So she began taking tea and cakes at five o'clock and inviting a few friends.

A lunch of bread and cheese

after a good walk is more enjoyable

than a Lord Mayor's feast.

Sir John Lubbock

There's nothing worth the wear of winning, but laughter and the love of friends.

HILAIRE BELLOC

Kindness in words creates confidence. Kindness in thinking creates profoundness. Kindness in giving creates love.

LAO-TSE

Wise sayings often fall on barren ground; but a kind word is never thrown away.

SIR ARTHUR HELPS

Friendship—our friendship—

is like the beautiful shadows of

evening, Spreading and growing

till life and its light pass away.

MICHAEL VITKOVICS

The hot water is to remain upon it
(the tea) no longer than while you can
say the Miserere Psalm (Psalm 51)
very leisurely.

SIR KENELM DIGBY

Love

Though weary, love is not tired;
Though pressed, it is not straitened;
Though alarmed, it is not confounded.
Love securely passes through all.

THOMAS À KEMPIS

*W*hen you love someone,
you love the whole person,
just as he or she is,
and not as you would like
them to be.

LEO TOLSTOY

Life is not so short but that
there is always time for courtesy.

RALPH WALDO EMERSON

God has put something noble
and good into every heart
His hand created.

MARK TWAIN

We do not make friends as we make houses, but discover them as we do the arbutus, under the leaves of our lives, concealed in our experience.

WILLIAM RADER

Many persons have a wrong idea about what constitutes true happiness. It is not attained through self-gratification, but through fidelity to a worthy purpose.

HELEN KELLER

Your wealth is where your friends are.

LATIN PROVERB

He who is plenteously provided for from within needs but little from without.

JOHANN WOLFGANG VON GOETHE

While more than 500 coffeehouses existed in London in the late seventeenth century, by 1717 Thomas Twining had opened the first gathering house strictly for tea. Women were also now welcomed, and tea soon became the most popular non-alcoholic beverage in England.

I think that love is the only spiritual power that can overcome the self-centeredness that is inherent in being alive. Love is the thing that makes life possible or, indeed, tolerable.

ARNOLD TOYNBEE

Live near to God and so all things will appear to you little in comparison with eternal realities.

ROBERT MURRAY McCHEYNE

*Do not anxiously hope
for that which is not yet come;
do not vainly regret
what is already past.*

Proverb

It is a good and safe rule to sojourn in every place as if you meant to spend your life there, never omitting an opportunity of doing a kindness, or speaking a true word, or making a friend.

JOHN RUSKIN

In 1904, "iced tea" was invented at the St. Louis World's Fair when an extreme heat wave caused patrons to forsake their customary cup of tea. In desperation, tea vendors added ice and offered it as a summer cooler. The rest, as they say, is history.

*W*here there is no extravagance
there is no love, and where there is
no love there is no understanding.

OSCAR WILDE

*B*est friend, my well-spring in the
wilderness!

GEORGE ELIOT

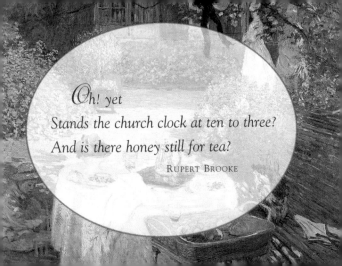

Oh! yet

Stands the church clock at ten to three?

And is there honey still for tea?

RUPERT BROOKE

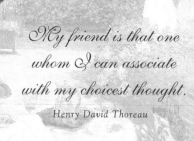

*My friend is that one
whom I can associate
with my choicest thought.*

Henry David Thoreau

*The happiest business in all the world
   is that of making friends;
And no investment on the street pays
   larger dividends,
For life is more than stocks and bonds,
   and love than rate percent,
And he who gives in friendship's name
   shall reap what he has spent.*

ANNE S. EATON

They are never alone that are accompanied with noble thoughts.

Sir Philip Sidney

One loyal friend is worth ten thousand relatives.

Euripides

We can only have the highest happiness by having wide thoughts, and much feeling for the rest of the world, as well as ourselves.

GEORGE ELIOT

The Book of Tea

The first Book of Tea was written by Lu Yu (A.D. 733-804) after five years of research. The detailed compendium made him a revered celebrity in China.

There is not a heart but has its moments of longing, yearning for something better, nobler, holier than it knows now.

HENRY WARD BEECHER

Kindness is a language which the deaf can hear and the blind can read.

MARK TWAIN

Above all else, guard your heart, for it is the wellspring of life.

PROVERBS 4:23

*O*ften we can help each other the
most by leaving each other alone;
at other times we need the hand-grasp
and the word of cheer.

ELBERT HUBBARD

*Love is a fabric
which never fades, no
matter how often it is washed
in the waters of adversity
and grief.*

Now stir the fire,
*   and close the shutters fast,*
Let fall the curtains,
*   wheel the sofa round;*
And while the bubbling
*   and loud hissing urn*
Throws up a steamy column,
*   and the cups,*

That cheer but not inebriate,
  wait on each,
So let us welcome peaceful evening in.

WILLIAM COWPER

Your house will look better if you decorate it with friends. They are the ornaments that will give it more attraction and cheer than all others combined. Nothing is comparable to the living ornaments that breathe so much warmth into plain quarters.

In the years prior to the American Revolution, patriotic colonists gave up tea abruptly and completely, even if the tea had been honestly smuggled into the country with no duty paid to the British.

Great works do not always lie in our way, but every moment we may do little ones excellently, that is, with great love.

FRANCIS OF SALES

There are evergreen men and women in the world, praise be to God!—not many of them, but a few. The sun of our prosperity makes the green of their friendship no brighter, the frost of our adversity kills not the leaves of their affection.

JEROME K. JEROME

Be Content

If solid happiness we prize,
Within our breast the jewel lies,
And they are fools who roam:
The world has nothing to bestow;
From our own selves our joys must flow,
And that dear place—our home.

*Life begins each morning....
Each morning is the open door
to a new world—new vistas,
new aims, new tryings.*

LEIGH HODGES

Don't Hurry

Don't hurry. When making tea you have only time. Let tea be a refuge, a genuine change of pace. Brewing your tea is part of drinking it and drinking it part of your life. Let the tea gently *stimulate you to reflect on how the smallest part touches and is touched by the infinite.*

THE BOOK OF COFFEE AND TEA

Everyone must have felt that a
cheerful friend is like a sunny day,
which sheds its brightness on
all around.

LORD AVEBURY

*L*ove is never lost. If not reciprocated it will flow back and soften and purify the heart.

WASHINGTON IRVING

A friend is worth all hazards we can run.

EDWARD YOUNG

America's love of tea began before the British ever arrived. In 1674, when New Amsterdam became New York under British rule, the colony probably drank more tea than all of England.

The true friend seeks to give, not to take; to help, not to be helped; to minister, not to be ministered unto.

WILLIAM RADER

To be able to look back upon one's past life with satisfaction is to live twice.

MARTIAL

The happiest moments my heart knows are those in which it is pouring forth its affections to a few esteemed characters.

THOMAS JEFFERSON

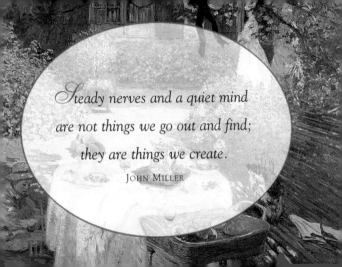

Steady nerves and a quiet mind

are not things we go out and find;

they are things we create.

JOHN MILLER

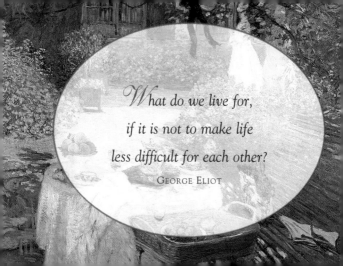

What do we live for,

if it is not to make life

less difficult for each other?

GEORGE ELIOT

If you are cold, tea will warm you—
If you are heated, it will cool you—
If you are depressed,
    it will cheer you—
If you are excited, it will calm you.

WILLIAM E. GLADSTONE

*My friends have come
to me unsought.
The great God gave them to me.*

Ralph Waldo Emerson